My Behaviour
I Can Help

Liz Lennon

W
FRANKLIN WATTS
LONDON • SYDNEY

Every day I do something to help my family.

When I get up, I make my bed.

When I lift the
sheets, I imagine
I'm floating!

I like playing
with my toys.

When I've finished,
I put them away.

I help to
look after
our dog.

I make sure he has water to drink.

Helping out in the garden is fun.

I have my own gloves and trowel!

I help Dad to
bake cakes.

Afterwards,
we clear up
together.

In the summer we pick raspberries and strawberries.

I race my brother to pick the most!

I help in the supermarket.

I put our food in the trolley.

At tea-time, I help my big sister set the table.

After tea,
I wipe
the table
clean.

I pretend
I'm a pirate
washing
a ship!

Mum is happy when I help.

Dad is happy when I help.
It feels nice to help.

About this book

It is important for young children to begin helping out in small ways to lay the groundwork for chores in later life. The aim of this book is to give you the opportunity to share and discuss different aspects of how they can help. Looking at and talking about the pictures is a good starting point. Here are a few ideas for activities and talking points.

Looking after themselves Making their own bed and putting away their toys are good tasks for every child. You could introduce a sticker chart to get them excited about helping.

Pets Helping out with pets is a good way to introduce responsibility. Talk about what animals need: food, water, warmth and exercise, and how pets rely on their owners to provide this.

Gardening and cooking These are things that many children enjoy and may not need to be persuaded to help with. If children are old enough to cook, they can also help to clear up. Why do we need to wash and put things away? Talk about why we put gardening equipment away - what might happen if we didn't?

Supermarket Some children enjoy shopping but others find it more of a chore. You could suggest they play games such as asking their parents for 'shopping lists' with little pictures on for them to find and tick off together.

Tea-time Helping out with setting the table or cleaning up after tea or wiping up after tea is a good time for children to help out so there is a sense of all the family pulling together.

First published in 2011
by Franklin Watts

Copyright © Franklin Watts 2011

Franklin Watts
338 Euston Road
London NW1 3BH

Franklin Watts Australia
Level 17/207 Kent Street
Sydney, NSW 2000

All rights reserved.

Printed in China

Series Editor: Sarah Peutrill
Art Director: Jonathan Hair
Series Designer: Paul Cherrill
Picture Researcher: Diana Morris
Consultants: Karina Philip
and Deborah Cox

Franklin Watts is a division of
Hachette Children's Books,
an Hachette UK company.

www.hachette.co.uk

Dewey number: 158.2'5
ISBN: 978 1 4451 0473 7

Picture credits:
Fotolia: matka Warlatka 7. Istockphoto: Dzhamiliya Ermakova 5; PK-Photos 9. Shutterstock: Avava 2; Brberrys 8; Kzenon front cover, 10; Morgan Lane Photography 1, 22; macka 11; Monkey Business Images 12, 23; Marcel Moolj 20; Juriah Mosin 14; O6photo 16; oliveromg 3; Poznyakov 6; Cory Thoman 21. Superstock: age footstock 15; Blend Images 13, 17; Fancy Collection 4; Image Source 18-19. Every attempt has been made to clear copyright. Should there be any inadvertent omission please apply to the publisher for rectification.

Index of English Names